HEAVEN

CENTS

Janie Peterson
Molly Zach

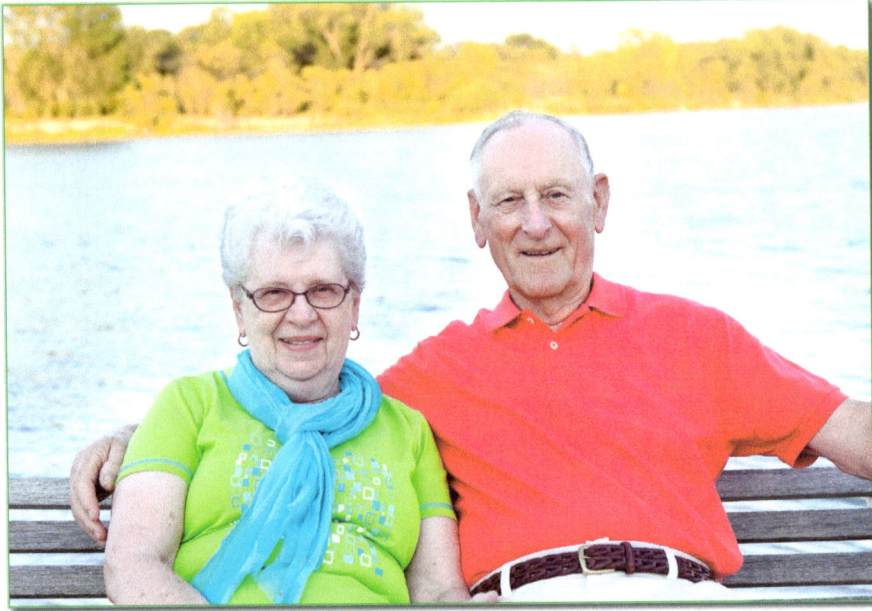

Lu and Elmer
My parents and spiritual role models.

HEAVEN CENTS

Janie Peterson

Molly Zach

BEHAVEN KIDS.

www.BehavenKids.com

Omaha, NE

HEAVEN CENTS
Text and illustrations ©2014 Janie Peterson

Published by Behave'n Kids Press Inc.
8922 Cuming St.
Omaha, NE 68114
(402) 926-4373
www.BehavenKids.com

Children's Paperback ISBN: 978-0-9714405-4-8
Adult's Paperback ISBN: 978-0-9714405-5-5

Library of Congress Cataloging Number: 2014937202

Publisher's Cataloging-in-Publication Data on file with the publisher

Project coordination by Concierge Marketing Publishing Services

Illustrations by Mike Pflaum

Printed in the United States of America
10 9 8 7 6 5 4 3 2

A church is a special place
where you come to pray
and be close to Jesus.

1

It is time for Church.

3

Elmer and Lu ran out of their rooms
ready for Church. Lu was dressed in pink,
with her play sewing kit slung over her
shoulder. She knew her mom would
be happy that she had picked
a quiet toy for Church.

Elmer had on his favorite red shirt, pants and ball hat. He carried his bat, glove, and ball. He was ready, too.

Dad hugged Elmer and let him know he loved his clean clothes, but that his bat, glove and ball were not right for Church. Dad asked Elmer to find another quiet toy to bring along and they would play ball when they came home.

Elmer trotted back to find a quiet toy. This time he returned with a deck of cards. Dad smiled, "This is a much better, quiet choice."

Mom and dad were smiling from
ear to ear this morning. They said they
had a special new plan called Heaven Cents.
This would help Elmer and Lu be good
and stay quiet in Church.

In the car, mom explained...

Heaven Cents

It's time to go to Church today.
My family likes to go and pray.
It's fun to get all clean and dressed,
To show God I'm at my very best.

At Church Mom says I must be quiet.
She has a plan, and I will try it.
And Daddy says he'll watch and see
How well behaved I can be.

I will whisper, play quiet and be good
I'll sing and pray like I should
With each whisper I'll get a penny, nickel or dime.
I hope they notice every time!

We call the coins our Heaven Cents
The more I'm quiet, the more I get.
I have an envelope that states my name
It's where my coins go, each time the same.

When the collection basket passes by me,
I'll put my envelope in as quiet as can be.
I'm so proud that I earned coins for being good,
And I gave it to God, just like Dad said I could.

Each time I go to Church I know
Being still and quiet is the best way to go.
Every coin I earn makes me smile and nod,
Because my Heaven Cents are my gift to God.

Heaven Cents sounded great!
Elmer, Lu, Mom, and Dad all walked
into Church ready. They saw some
of their friends and said hello.

As they waited for the service to begin, Elmer took out his deck of cards and began playing quietly.

Mom reached into her pocket
and handed Elmer his first
penny. Elmer's eyes lit up.

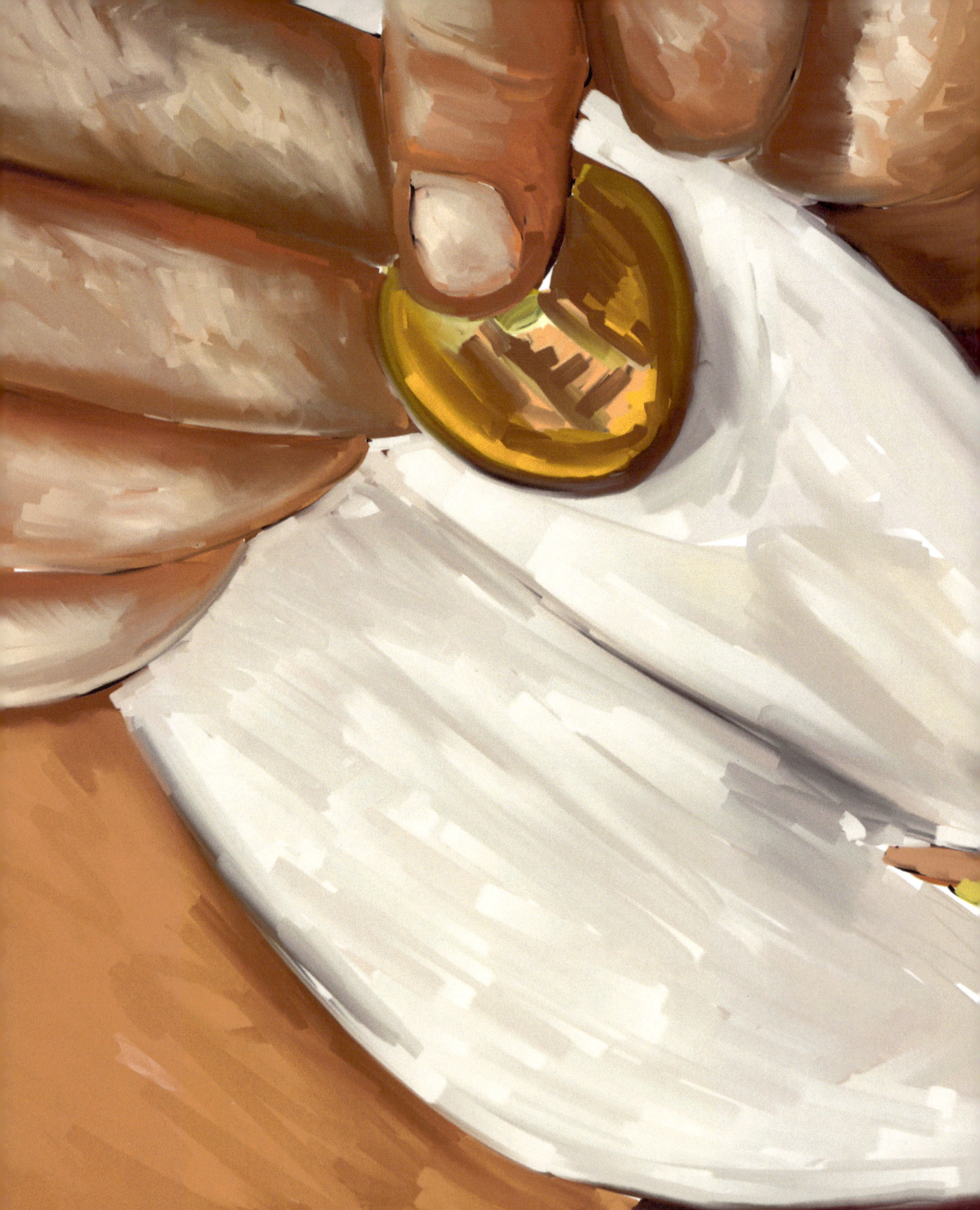

Elmer carefully placed his penny in the envelope with his name. Mom whispered, "You are playing very quietly!" He immediately went back to playing with his cards.

Lu was playing quietly with her sewing. Dad said, "Lu, you are sitting very still." He reached into his pocket for Lu's first penny. Lu smiled with delight, put the penny in her envelope and continued to play quietly.

Soon the service began.
Everyone was singing. Elmer and
Lu sang too. Dad slowly reached
into his pocket again and gave
Elmer and Lu more Heaven Cents.

Mom whispered to each child
how proud she was that
they were singing.

When the basket was passed for the collection, Elmer and Lu sealed their envelopes and proudly put their earnings into the basket. Mom and Dad then took out the extra envelopes so that Elmer and Lu could begin filling them with more coins.

Elmer and Lu earned many Heaven Cents and many praises from Mom and Dad. They kept a quiet whispering voice, they didn't wiggle and squirm too much, they sang songs, they prayed, they even shared their toys.

When services were over, Mom
and Dad took Elmer and Lu up
to the basket to drop off their
second filled envelopes. Mom
and Dad were so proud of
their children's manners
during Church.

When they went outside, Mom and Dad picked up Elmer and Lu and twirled them in the air with joy. Mom and Dad's friends noticed how quiet they were, too.

Elmer and Lu beamed!

28

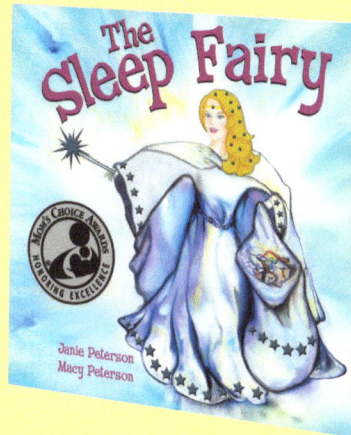

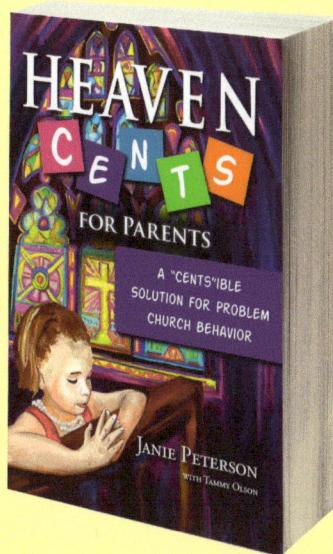

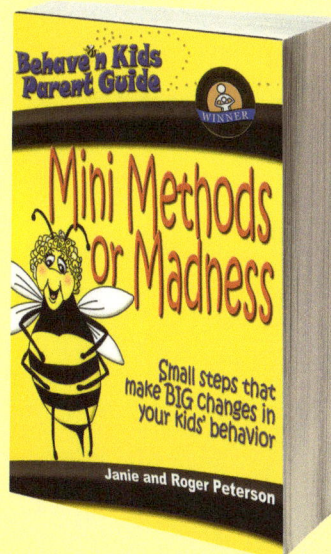

www.ingramcontent.com/pod-product-compliance
Lightning Source LLC
Chambersburg PA
CBHW042126040426
42450CB00002B/90